MONSTER-PROOF POETRY

JUDYMAY MURPHY

MONSTER-PROOF POETRY

 EYEWEAR PUBLISHING

First published in 2019
by Eyewear Publishing Ltd
Suite 333, 19-21 Crawford Street
Marylebone, London W1H 1PJ
United Kingdom

Cover design and typeset by Edwin Smet
Author photograph by Irmantas Bauza (Black& white photo),
XJG photography and Susie Hemsworth (Colour cover photo)

Printed in England by TJ International Ltd, Padstow, Cornwall

ISBN 978-1-912477-91-3

WWW.EYEWEARPUBLISHING.COM

To you,
for sticking around to
grow even more monster-proof daily.

I've known Judymay to wear
several hats over several years — all of them
stylishly. But here, as a poet, she thoughtfully
and touchingly encompasses all the Judymays
I've known and loved. Now it's your turn to get
to know and love her.

TIGGER!

TABLE OF CONTENTS

FOREWORD

People write, perform, read and listen to poetry for countless diverse reasons.

The poetry collected herein, *Monster-Proof Poetry*, is about realising that you have the ability and opportunity to obliterate the inner and outer monsters in your life. The hope is that it will inspire you to fully engage with the world in more powerful ways. It's designed to remind you that your dreams, triumphs and tribulations have been heard and are valid, no matter how you may have been buffeted about until now. It is especially for those softer souls who often feel demolished by the actions of pushy, shouty people and what can feel like endless encroachments into your more gentle assertions.

Samuel Beckett talked about every word being 'an unnecessary stain on silence...' But I believe that often the silence can be its own stain, that a lack of voice can damage you daily and in subtle ways. This silence gives the monsters full reign.

I'm interested, of course, in how a poem sounds to you and how it resonates linguistically, emotionally, musically... However, I'm far more interested in what a poem does, in who you are after having read it, what you do as a result of whatever's been stirred up in you. What action do you commit, to that might otherwise have lain stagnant and unstirred? Do you now choose to shake out some space for an old wound to heal, do you say 'no' to a damaging by a person or idea, do you now dare to go in for a delightful, blunderingly awkward kiss, do you wake up to your own wonder, do you finally find the part of you that has the courage to dream again or to walk out through a stoutly nailed door? Perhaps you simply make the next cup of tea with slightly greater style and aplomb, and that counts. This is where my being a motivational speaker and being a poet meet, at the place of: what can these words do for your actual experience of life? Hopefully I can help you to reimagine yourself as a powerful agent of change for the better.

Poetically I work within a stricter rhythmic structure and with many more rhymes and part-rhymes than may be deemed edgy or fashionable right now. I find these forms keep me disciplined while also helping you to digest and relate. That's just my choice and I make no claim as to it being superior or even valid – it's just my way. Being merely diverting, sentimental or clever has never been the point. Of anything.

Thanks for hanging out with me here. My dearest hope is that you meet yourself in new ways in these poems and start to sing back at monsters more wildly than ever before.

Judymay Murphy
London, 2019.

A DREAM IS A VERY LONG PIECE OF STRING

Your dream is no thirst for an unsalted spring,
Neither a distant far-happening land.
Some think it a kitten insistent to grow
To a blind naked rat, when a lion was planned,
Or a book of blank pages beyond Chapter Five,
Forsaken for rank-and-file daily demands.

A dream is quite simply a long length of string
Aching to wrap around winnable things,
Full casting to hook into half-crafted shapes,
Growing strong alongside before pulling them in.
But abandoned in pockets all strings limply wait,
Unravelled, frustrated, like small, untried wings.

It takes time to grow strong and more still to grow wise.
Though too tiny for hitching of wagons to stars
Let nobody laugh at your slight twist of thread,
For it's plenty enough for the binding of hearts.
As it muscles to metal, grown tempered by time,
Ever climbing past failing designs and false starts.

No a dream is not some punitive, eat-by-dated thing,
A dream is just a very long, yearning piece of string.

BEST NOT BOYFRIEND

We're like sister and big brother, was the deadly verbal knife,
Your social weapon of choice,
Marking me as very nearly worthy but not quite,
And wielded in your care-of-tiny-kittens kind of voice.

We've always been such good friends, was the dagger next to harm;
Your thrust against my need,
Impervious to all my wit, my parrying with charm,
Proving unrequited love to be a target soft indeed.

But drunk enough to want me at the waning of the night,
You open enough to exclaim,
We're more like second cousins or in-laws you and I,
I could do you but then Christmas would just never be the same.

Then by daybreak, *We're true soulmates*, you blithely acquiesce,
Your defences half demolished,
And though ready to be conquered, alas I can't forget
Your boastful stories of your smallsword and with whom you've
        had it polished.

So I'd rather be your sister/buddy/in-law/cousin/teacher
Than some battle-tale conceit.
Sweet duelling pistol pal of mine
You softly sodden creature,
I thank you for conceding, but my triumph is in my retreat.

A PICTURE

I've a portrait in my attic.
Not to age while I stay young,
Instead it shows the orphaned things
The better me might well have done.

Replete with hats I meant to wear
And miles of streets unstepped upon,
Pigmented smiles that never were,
Set free from all I left unsung.

These abstracts of dead destinies
Drip now with colours of the day,
Equipped to counteract the fact
Of my anaemic little way.

This picture of what might have been
(My hurt unpainted self can see)
Is worst in that it plainly shows
I might have done this all with ease.

My faded shoe upon the step,
And turning now, I hope one day,
Amid the smell of mice and dust,
To find it framing only grey.

THE AUL' TRIANGLE

I know you know that love's a curse,
That when your target sights another
Still you crave said longed-for lover.
Dear one, this triangle hurts,
I know you know the way it works.

I know you know love blinds all sight,
As you want me still once again
I long for him, while he wants men.
I know you turned him down last night,
You know my dear, triangles bite.

I know you know the way love is,
So, tired of faking hopes and smiles,
Let's settle on a compromise.
Come close my dear, the deal now is:
I'll show you mine if you show me his.

A LETTER OF POOR APOLOGY

When we grow old and gorged with days
You'll see your life writ plain and whole,
While I will gaze on fragments and
Sorting through the scattered sands,
I used to live in Ireland, I will say.

I felt that I could only leave
And skip the sod once more again,
Needing as I did the ease
Of New York's villages back then,
Where I could breathe the old town from my lungs.

While in brave bars and basements
From Ballymun to Capel Street,
You who kept your accent strong
Drew dominion from the botch,
While I grew softer under memory.

Like coats of me I left behind,
Some tender ghost that long remains
Toward the stranded tides of sea,
Clamoured on a bench with friends.
A daughter of Dublin's fair difficulty.

As I pack my small belonging
To pitch the circus someplace new,
And dine out on my Irishness,
I stole your riches, I confess –
I drank the Liffey dry before I left.

A STONE IS NOT A SEED

You gifted me a part of what you could;
A tiny stone from gardens richly proud.
You daily set before my starveling plate
A mocking little pebble from dry ground.

I learned to look for nothing but the small,
The least of every offering to hand.
I'd turn inside to eat in silent hate,
Quieting my hunger, tilling promised land.

I'd bite the stone, and people would just look
And wonder, *Why so sad this young a face?*
Not knowing that our food is what we are,
Making me a meagre little stone of deepest grey.

SOHO

The world's too much for this one heart,
The loud too loud, the falling foul.
It's always never easy
All about the bars in pleasure town.

Still less so all around the mind,
That littered pavement of the night;
The stubbings and the spillages,
Unwilling yet to quiet down.

It's always later in the day,
But still I'm stuck to craven rooms,
My coat too thin to brave the air,
My boots too bloated with the rain.

My God's too short, my world too wide,
My tribe too flung for gathering;
So, taught too well by luckless cats,
I wait until the dark to sing –

And pray that soon the sickened street
Will sink me to illicit sleep,
For it's always far too *something*
When you drink the outside in.

ICE-CREAM DAYS

Today,
Out of a lazy, not much moment,
I remembered how my Mother
Used to take up my ice-cream
And lick away swiftly the melting parts,
To render it doable once again
For my eager little hands
And awkward mouth.
Then I remembered
Those who never knew such things,
Nor even such a day as one
To expect an ice cream in.
And then my mind went to those
Who never knew where they were from,
And I felt unbearably happy for myself,
And then happy and ridiculously sad for us all.
And that's when the tears
Started falling strong.

HAT

A well-worn blue woollen hat
That might well belong to you.
Sodden with sand and encrusted
And found in a seawater pool.

Salted with ages all faded,
Now a home for some hermited thing
That creeps out all in a bubble,
To pull back, forgoing to swim.

This hat died from far too much thinking
I realise, stopping to stare,
Shoving my hands deep in pockets,
The wind playing bird with my hair.

Is the hat finally silent,
Dripping the soak of the sea?
I wonder you wore it so long,
And hope you're away swimming free.

AFTER GOD'S SILENCE

Your bellyheart will fill once more
My love, I promise that.
The skinnied vine around your door
Will plump, and run to fat.
This ringing nothing from the skies
Shall one day rain as sound,
While hollow hells of lows and highs
Shall plane to greater ground.
Such sorrowing of 'not enough'
Is born to fall undone,
And I shall sing you soup, my love,
Until your harvest comes.

AND SO MERRY CHRISTMAS

So a puppy is not just for Christmas I know,
Although some people are, some people like you.
Though sweatered in stories you knitted with rage
Here's what I'd say if I were built brave, in fact,
Here's what I'd get as a facial tattoo –

I am not broken, it's your eye that's bent,
Your deaf ear no proof that my song has no tune.
Far from the wrongness you need me to be,
I'm no longer wide open for slicing in two,
I'm alive and I'm strong and now strangely immune.

You're hot-weather human mittens at best,
At worst the oblivious venom in tea,
And still you keep pouring your odious self
All over what's left of the brightest of me,
Ever holding my hand as if stemming a bleed.

So it's not that I'm weak, for all fighters would tire
Of your notional construct of how I should live,
Going fifty-odd rounds over old cups of woe
As I wrestle the 'me' and the 'mine' from your grip.
(I'd say) it's not my job to forget or forgive.

Restricted emotions now ribboned in ink –
Merry Christmas.
I'm keeping the puppy I think.

SPHERE

When they note that your eyes are two differing shades,
One for each realm, you abstrusely explain,
One for the sorrow and one for the bliss.
Thereafter they question, *So then, which is which?*
Herein lies the lesson, a truth you know well –
My Sweetness, you must always save your bluest eye for Hell.

THE LADY OF THE MERRION

In this place where turf and wood-fed flame
Touch soft the tripping sound of teas and spoons,
Where dripping chandelier and aged mirror
Mirror back the aching afternoon.

In this place where servers from far seas
Set firm the sugars fast upon the tray,
Wherein each half-lost girl spills history
From silver pots of chocolate and earl grey.

In this place where lives the Lavery fair,
All powdered grey-white face as fires burn,
While men of 23 spark fresh coals there,
Killing her with talk of rates and terms.

In this place invasion comes by day,
In rain-macked groups that coarsely hack the bloom
From proud chrysanthemums, and on they stay,
Too casual, too loud for such a room.

A gap in time itself sits in this house,
Bridged perhaps by ages under frame.
So was I this Lady once and am I still?
In this place of gentle haunting, of tea, and turf, and rain.

THE GATHERED

Suited and groomed and so gathered they were,
The men of the money, the counts and their queens,
Backless and strapless and slathered in fur,
The woman he chose but had never quite seen.

Spirits in spirits for drowning the ill,
Her longings ignored and pushed back from her face,
The cut of the dress and the numb of the pill,
The violin whispered, *You're in the wrong place.*

Duty, she'd claim, was her chain and her hope,
Her prayers pouring out to be roundingly spilled,
As that night he tied her with more pretty rope
As he slipped on her bones a new bracelet of gilt.

Seated and eated and drunken they grew,
The men of the moment now voices full sound,
Around them contingencies, clusters and slew,
And there, on the edge, sits our haute couture gown.

Voluntary prey has nowhere to hide
So out they parade and then indoors they cry,
Homeless in houses with gates on each side,
Too late to be lovely, too early to die.

Plucked and adored and discarded they lie
The women of men who live only to build,
Yet no man of stature can understand why
He finds himself tied to a thing that he killed.

Then half-fed, re-groomed and gathered again,
Dead women will smile to beguile empty men.

BREAD

I raged against my tiny life,
I wrote anew the master scheme,
And prayed an answer to come quick,
To fix my mediocrity.

Writing fast on gravied napkins,
Hopes of houses, fame and ease,
I pushed away my empty plate,
To make room for my plan to breathe.

Then my sated eye caught sight of
One forsaken piece of bread.
Bread half-tasted, half-forgot,
The luxury of those full-fed.

My pen then dropped as if to rouse
My unsuspecting heart and head
And, stopping for a moment,
My dreaming set to start afresh.

Today I build my latest castle
Grateful in my wakening,
Knowing that uneaten bread
Is half the planet's greatest dream.

ON MENTAL HUSBANDRY

I have married one hundred, hundred men,
Married mostly on the train and on the bus,
Pried from sodden books and dusty movies then
Head-wed and over long before the next stop.
A transporting addiction since the awkward age of ten,
A mind awash with soldiers groomed and shot.

I have married a host of troops complete,
A hundred thousand men my love brought low,
Causing me to wonder did I flag my own defeat,
Rejecting gentlemen of heat and blood and bone.
Did I pass him on the street last year, last week,
And was I far too busy marrying to know?

I have married a million, million more,
Now littering the beaches of my brain,
And I the one true victim of this single journey war,
Still I sing *I do, I do, I take this train.*
And with every pledge of love that is pedestrian and sure,
I wave my white veil overhead and plead insane.

THE SETTLE

Perishing cold a traveller heeds
The constant call of an open fire.
With blackened motes from tinder sticks
Piloting a twist of smoke,
Kindled and coaxed to a blue red core,
Inglenook of your own desire –
Heaven the books that quiet the soul,
The feeling of the endless possibility of toast.

Lullabied home by burning flame,
Your mission unmet on the unfinished road,
Triumph unknown but belly well fed,
With wild roving tamed and vaguely postponed.
Hear the whistle of sap in its final breath
As the tree of your summer breaks into death.
Draw back from the fire my comforted friend,
For that which warms consumes you, cremates you in the end.

TO ANOTHER'S PERFECTION

If my lips could hold to red like yours,
My legs would lengthen too, I'm sure.
Perhaps I'd start to fold my arms
In ways less awkwardly demure.
If my mouth but formed a perfect bow,
My breath would soften, blink would slow,
Harvesting admiring men,
I'd dance with caution wildly thrown.
I'd chance to silence, being you,
Free from panicked urge to prove
(With witty phrase, with surging angst)
My wherewithal to live-up-to.
If I were of your blessèd tribe
Of women who were born arrived
With ribboned waist and easy hip,
My lips would ache with wanton might,
So much adored, each man unmade.
And yet, I find it somehow strange
That only in the human horde
The hunted ones live unafraid
While I remain obscure and pale.
Yes, my lips would love to red like yours.

CHAPTER

Walk away, walk away –
Pack your lessons under arm
In a satchel filled with freedom waxed by grief.

Say your silent goodbyes
To the dead and never-lived.
Do not dare to thank them as you leave.

Walk away, walk away –
For life was never here,
Brave champion of burgeoning belief!

Set your newly certain eye
On the unlit road ahead,
With neither sun nor stars to bring relief.

Walk away, walk away –
For life lies through the trees,
Where you'll meet yourself but softer, your Calvary complete.

LOVE SICKENING STILL

It starts not with a needle
Nor a glass of sickly rum
But a glance that seems to offer
To undo the damage done.
A rush of promised respite
From the pain you can't outrun,
But the love you never got is always gone.

It kicks in through the dreaming bone
And soon enough succumbs
To echoes of old hungers
Ungrieved and bleeding strong.
So where you hoped for feeding
You're only sucking crumbs.
For the love you never got is always gone.

SLOWLY SUMMER ON A STEP

It was a night when breathing deep
Was like drinking all the soups
Of the streets and the corner slabs
And the groups of half-connected friends
Who asked each other what the plan was
And doing so then became the plan.
And stopping low on a brownstone stoop
Became as much like music on
Those lazy still-bright stretches as when
Lightnin' Hopkins used to play guitar.

An ice-cold glass of anything
Soon grows sweated as the rest.
A woman thinks she hears her name but,
Thighs too damp in her last year's dress,
She chooses not to go see,
Instead running her dream about owning a bar
(Somehow losing an hour on this)
And starts to guess that nights like these
Don't wish to let her win the world –
A night for dogs that dare not bark
A night for swimless fish and hapless girls.

THE LAZARUS DEVICE

Death is temporary –
Yours, I mean.
You will rise from your stale-sheeted bed,
To fillet your heart, kick start your head
And then ask where it was that you went for a while.
Why did you sleep when the fair was in town
When the ride could be so worth the risk?
Now breathe a little (if you dare)
And realise affliction is a cunning little gift
Not cashable for careless ease
Or honey in your handsome fist.
Death (your Death) is done for now, so
Allow the fates to breakfast on the action that you take –
Rip up the rules
Recast the day
Grit the very sky
And bin the chances missed as more come rolling into play.
Death is largely optional (at least for you and I)
So don't daub your desperate autograph on days not fully done.
Now ditch the shroud of shopworn trance that kept you playing small
And rise to drag your darling self across the unswept floor –
And play the hand that's dealt you
Aces high and spades to draw,
As Death bows low to honour you – you freakish, freshly born.

THE VISIT

I dreamed last night you knew me,
The decades all delayed,
I stepped into a space where time
Will softly turn away.
And in that very softly place,
I dreamed you knew my name.

I dreamed you asked me calmly,
Are we now writing still?
And my reply, *Indeed we are –*
Just as we always will
Then dreamed an echo of your eyes
And breathed again my fill.

Last night I dreamed you knew me,
Before the dogs of mind
Were freed to slip their ropes and run
To ground my snatch of time.
And I now empty leave to hope
You'll one day dream in kind.

A bruised and tiny self inside
Knows well that if you stay
Your broken words will point a path,
A yet unbeaten way.
So tonight, I'll dream you know me,
And fail to wake for day.

ON STANDING TOO CLOSE

The vast length of half of a lifetime
And another twenty odd yards,
And (as with then) the right amount
Of awkwardness standing its guard.

Seeing you there leaves me seeking
In your life-ridden jacket and jaw,
In each care-eaten singular gesture,
For the him, for the you of before.

While guessing in me you're expecting
That wry teenage mess you once met,
Smudged eyes and raw legs hung at angles,
Your too young unstrung marionette.

I'm surely her triumphal shadow,
And you the great keeper of him,
And so we land late in the game
Still not knowing how to begin.

I once would curse oceans between us,
Yet now it's the time that seems hard,
For half a life feels somehow longer
Than some half million miles of mere yards.

BILLY LIAR

Flotsam of scrapbooks of notional times
Ripped from imagining, glued to his mind.
Not normal, and yet not the sectioning kind
Of mental offences, just life left behind.

Strange all the townsfolk, still stranger the town,
So he built his own country of gorgeous renown
In his head, and he goes to this marvellous land
To lock out the noise, leaving love on remand.

Do you have a world where you go when you're gone?
Would you change here for there and live lies all day long
To candy the bitter, to ease your sweet tooth?
And is it pure weakness if there you feel strong?
And is it called lying if truer than truth?

CONCERT

Am I now more of a missing
From the crush of heaving shore,
That aching crest of certain death
Of sweated press and wrested arm
Reaching hard with urgent breath
From the wreck of an unstalled heart?
Am I now more of a missing
Where once I scored my sacred place
Among the masses and the horde
Braving of their surge toward you?
Not so much a crowd but more
A loud, a long, a rogue embrace.
And (though soft swallowed by the world)
My blood still tastes that nascent wave,
Urging me to that same space,
To be no longer missing, and far less afraid.

WHENEVER YOU SEEM TO BE GONE

If I could draw you back again
It wouldn't be
To listen to
Your whisper from the grave –

Nor to excite some wistful game
Of looking back
Through books of life
Already packed away –

And neither would I press on you
That empty pause
Of recent days
The pain now caused by death –

Should you appear one sudden day
I'd not so much
As touch your face
Nor hang upon your mouth –

Instead I'd sit and close my eyes
And love you more,
So very like
You'll find me doing even now.

ON BESIEGING, BEING SO BESIEGED

Dear God, I ask one thing of you –
I mean to say, one small thing more
(Knowing well how much I fail
To feel, to see, to thank you for).

Dear God, I don't want scratch-card stuff,
The dream rolled in, the storehouse filled,
I don't ask to be gifted with
The things you gave me hands to build.

Dear God, this ask is small yet wide.
I want one Great Obsession please.
If you would send me on a quest,
Or swell me with some raging need.

And God, this thing to rule my days,
I ask that it have not the smell
Nor shape, nor touch nor taste of men
As such obsession ends in… Well –

Dear God it keeps me sad and poor
So please Dear God, Dear God above,
Do send me a mission,
Just don't make it Love.

GLADLY

If I could hold your hurt away I would,
And you so softly breathing through the bile.
I'd lie to you and paint a world so good,
If just to stem your bleeding soul a while.

If I could sing your life away I'd gladly,
Lullabies of ease and endless glories,
And stand my guard so crazy, deeply, madly,
That reality would cave and read you stories.

UNFIXED RATES OF INTEREST

Thank you, thank you! Yes!
I am indeed that restless stray
Famed in straighter circles
For my... let's say
My impeccable taste in impossible men.

That tribe of the torridly respectable,
Who seldom deign to buy but
Still shop like a walking lottery win.
As they bottle my worth to sample at whim,
As they vouchsafe me kindly my own self esteem,
As I start to expend my joie-de-damn-vivre
By holding my opinions and stomach muscles in.

Fast forward the tale,
But not too far
(And not even too much faster than it lives.)
And, figurative top-hat doffed
And numbers blocked from thwarted phones,
Now they act as if my weeping
Were something that I cared
To come up with all on my own.

Run along, shiny men
And play properly,
Or at least elsewhere.
For I'm spent now from owing well-nigh all of me
To the bank of those so blind they'll never see.

I reserve the right fully to fool myself,
To cause my desires to be clumsily dashed,
To prettily lie to my credulous self.
However, from now on –
All others pay cash.

WANTING FOR WORD

Let me know I still exist.
A word to break this silent weather.
Speak me to that safer shore
Where love may kiss me back together.

Save me with a moment's thought,
Some line to drag me feathers first
From the wasteland of this wait
This hopeful nothing of a curse.

Let me know my heart still beats
And is not lying dead somewhere,
Rescue swift and send me peace;
Pen a lifeline, breathe me air.

FLOCK

I figured God to be a morning person,
Something the cafe owner understood,
Setting me a table and chair outdoors
For we are like family, those who wake at dawn
To impose slow handprints on the fresh day –
The farmers, sweepers, ready-makers,
The poets of more sanguine, sober ways.

This cobbled square is where I'd go
Hoping He'd be coming out to play,
(For though God thought churches were fairly okay
He declared they weren't really His scene.)
As usual He was away curbing zeal,
So He sent a perfect herald, a prophet with wings –
A sparrow to teach me how to pray.

Having no schedule she perched near my cup
In the almost sun and merging shade,
Not dwelling on how there was no food to take,
Just hopping on up the chair-back and then
Watching for nothing, and waiting for nothing again.
I prayed that I too could hope to know
That the world might hold without my furious grip.

BOY WRITER

How is it you can be so young
And yet so very ashen,
With liver spent and mind undone
And beer in place of passion?

Why is it you were sent to me
All burning dull with promise,
To lay your brilliance at my feet
And then proceed to vomit?

Oh vandal sweet, my fetid one,
All smoke and ink and sighing.
How is it you can be so young
And yet so very dying?

CO-DEPENDENT HOBBIES

Your hobbies are hikes, and things on bikes
And baking and playing guitar.
Others like skating and preening and painting
And picnicking trips in the car.
I spend my days (I'm sad to report)
Presuming my futures with dread,
Impressing the quite unimpressible sorts,
And saving the already dead.
That done I'll start on your laundry,
The dirty, full-metaphored kind,
I'll then do your washing while constantly wishing
For easier ways to unwind.
If you love online games or to jog in the rain
Then I envy the ease of your way,
For my time is all moping and yearning and hoping
That I might somehow, maybe,
End up with a life
That is mostly more 'me' and less 'they'.

BLANKET FORT

I'm a blanket fortress person,
All sag and soft and just enough
For staving off the lightest of
Daily frost and slightest rain.

I built me tens of years ago
From parts of you that seemed too much –
Too high a bar, too crooked a frame,
And books that you said not to touch.

Unlikely as this fort may be
(My rugged keep, a lumpen lair)
At least my hurt is housed within
This place where witness cannot bear.

And on I grow a leery fort,
For shame is adverse to the light,
And here I hold my brittle self
And pray you'll ease it back to life.

And each and every empty day,
When you do not arrive again,
I crawl and close the blanket door,
And eat stale biscuits from the tin.

But hiding isn't why I'm here,
So one day very soon I hope
I'll take up all my brittle bits
And make from my fortress
A boat.

ON THE KEEPING OF PEOPLE

I recommend you cultivate a pet,
A creature nestled whining at your knee,
A blend of friend and animal and guest,
Of stunningly pathetic pedigree.
You only need to feed them discontent,
With short leads round the bend up garden paths to lunacy.

Find someone trained up by years of pain,
And mind you promise more than you provide,
Then substituted for true love again,
Your muttley pet will doggedly comply.
Kept to heel with masterful disdain,
With pocketfuls of maybe, sweet-treated out with smiles.

Beware, beware, the weary beast may turn,
Take care the day your social spare departs,
And runs into the arms of one who yearns
For all that you discounted from the start.
Leaving you to curse your lessons learned,
With 'Missing' posters stapled to your tiny little heart.

HOME

I live in the house next door to myself –
Such a head-sore, exhausting way to be,
With occasional dutiful trips back from there
To check that the mould of the mind doesn't creep,
That the floors aren't contorting to ceilings,
That old jumble is reasonably stored.

Living in the house next door to yourself
Finds you baking for praise, playing almost your tunes,
Spinning out proof that you own the parade
For the transients who traipse through your rooms
To get a button or a smile sewn on,
Having heard that you give yourself for free.

Sometimes when you sit in your house next door
A latent heat comes pleading through the wall,
Ignored by you till it grows by degrees
Unbearable, too much for your design.
Only then do you rush back to see
Whether or not you have simply
Burned to the ground.

THE FOLDEN

Alone I am complete until
Your gutting voice your
Yawning requisition of all
The available space as yours.
All but entering me along
With the room, well so
Again I fold myself away
Like some piece of cheap umbrella.

Self-pleated and once more alone
In unremembered
Air-sick homes and forgotten,
The plain slice beside the buttered ones,
As being unobtrusive is
Mainly why slowly
I am suffered to survive
At half the size and full undone.

Fetched in for family occasions
No-one celebrates
The spare fold-out table they just
Praise one another on their
Foresight in allowing that the
Graceless item might
Be of use, then tidied away,
And I helpfully fold apace.

How I long to unravel in rolling hills
In a delicious lack of permission
To be a place where you cannot
and to say with all my body that I am
I am endless and actually full sized
and shall be remaining on generous display.

WORM INSIDE

There lives a kind of worm inside,
A worm of worry, small and blind.
A creeping, leeching little grub
That stops the heart and stalls the mind.
It slips you back to lower tenths,
With residues of thoughts unkind.

There lives a kind of worm inside,
With sucker ties that bind and block.
It sleeps in sugared goods until
Awakened by the bailiff's knock.
Then takes your breath, your very tongue,
And fixes one eye to the clock.

There lives a kind of worm that reigns,
Rides in on fear and owns the gut.
When tempered-ill the worm will gain,
A heart to silence, blood to rust.
So rout the beast with all you are
Before it eats your dreams to dust.

THE BODY AND HER DOG

Out from under the slippered feet
Of the housekeeper owned by the nuns,
Out a dog creeps from the warm winter corner
Of the seeping, mildewed, convent scullery heat.
Out because the morning clock threatens for eleven,
When a bleak air and fair promise
Drive onward the great black lollop of a beast,
And he winding up the yard of
The brightly Jesused school for the polite.

Its walls held together by old-lady prayers
And raffle tickets and paint just as ancient
And frail, and perhaps just as smelling of yellow.
The outside tract is tar, then sod, then stone,
A tricolor harsher than nature had planned.
Then like pullets amazed by a daily opened cage
Here they land, the far too much too many and the more,
Years before they'll have handed over
Their entire sense of self to a boy.

The ritual begins with the feeding of the dog
With their blessed little bits of break-time snack,
Until tired of their turn the gabardined girls
Stake their space between dirt-dusted, half-paid-for cars
(Parked by the staff in desultory rows)
All shouts to allot the sequence for the jumping of a rope.
Ad-hocked well enough from smaller lengths of knots
As their mothers had, their grandmothers, theirs…
Sometimes a washing line I think it was.

Daily the flock, the gaggle, the swarm
The makings of every perpetual norm,

51

Moving and weaving and laughing and leaping
And barking and feeding – All but one.

Stooped as if halting a fall from herself
And so utterly still beside the wheeling hound,
Faintly claiming the dog as her own,
(Or was it, I wonder, not the other way round?)
A young child of ninety or so it would seem, from her
Turtled back, her hungry restraint and acutely rag-doll knees.
Haunted gaze as if all she knew,
Piece by piece, had slowly died at war.

The girl the pivot, the dog the reel,
The pair would hold the pattern fast and wait,
Ignored and unsure and both stalled in their way,
He in an anti-Pavlovian fashion, she to hear time called
On that particular slice of the unlivable.
Until masking the sounds of workaday play
Bells muster the strewn into queues and then rooms.
Did the dog suppose her waiting for scraps of snacks of her own?
Or did he see her as she saw herself, as carrion for crows?

Different times, many would claim,
Since you hid your frigid hands in
Stretched cardigan sleeves on arctic mornings
Of frozen doorstep milk, of the hard-butter sandwiches
Squashed, missing or far away lost
Under school books and lack of actual care.
A good sized forever since your safety
Depended on the medal you miraculously wore,
Your health on a finger of water from Lourdes.

But time rides on, days turn around.
Up, under and then over like the one, two, three of the rope.
And here today she stands again, forty winters on.

Though most would have taken odds on the dog
Outlasting such a godforsaken slip of a thing,
Grown now into shapes just impressive enough
To itch at those who knew her way back when.
And her older, now unbitten lip speaks of a life well lived.

Not altered so much as reupholstered, I suppose,
As her stately gesture falters just enough
To show that she is not so worldly polished after all.
Her posture slipping from a shoulder now and then,
Caught and returned to acceptable forms.
Her muscles pulling hard, a contracting wolf within.
A faithful, steadfast, armoring beneath her fashion-house
Tanned and smiling limbs.
Braced for an ache she's already survived.

Primed for a pain that's been long since outlived –
For no number of days can hope to erase
The damage done to children left outdoors.
The brain forgets,
The heart forgives,
But the body keeps the score.

ADVANCING HEARTS

Oh, take heart!
Take *my* heart if yours
Is in for repairs,
For my heart knows things
That yours has forgot.
Unbarred from its bind
Mine softly dares
To summon up words
From lost corners of us.

My love, all is good,
It knowingly sings,
(Resowing the seeds
Of dreams you once owned)
Singing, *Buildings are simply*
Rubble that reached,
And birds are just
Eggs that have flown.

While time is just nothing
But oddly sliced pie,
A hero but an
Ounce of you full grown.
And rainbows far more than
Old colours that cried,
Though gentle rain is
Disappointed snow.

So and on it goes —
Mine sings to your heart!
Your fountain that dried
Your engine that could.

Not broken, only
Up on bricks nearby.
Tomorrow's fine kingdoms
You'll boldly make good
When your vision holds firm
Through my borrowed eye.

So have my hope if yours
Is sleeping tonight.
Take heart,
Take heart,
Take heart.

A READER'S KEY TO THE POEMS

'A Dream Is a Very Long Piece of String'
For anyone who's worried that they've left it too late to accomplish their dreams.

'Best Not Boyfriend'
When it hurts to have a friend with whom you'd rather be more than friends.

'A Picture'
Consolation for those who know they can achieve much more in life.

'The 'Aul Triangle'
You have the hots for someone who has the hots for someone else and so then...

'A Letter Of Poor Apology'
For anyone who ever ran away from home and is still running.

'A Stone Is Not A Seed'
For anyone who was chronically neglected at any stage.

'Soho'
If it feels as if the place you live is all too much some-times.

'Ice-Cream Days'
If your mother is weighing on your mind.

'Hat'
Specially for the over-thinkers.

'After God's Silence.'
For anyone needing reassurance that the future will be
better.

'And So Merry Christmas'
Full suit of armour against a toxic family member.

'Sphere'
Needing to remember that there are two sides to us all.

'The Lady Of The Merrion'
For whenever you wish to feel timeless.

'The Gathered'
For anyone deluded into wishing they could marry into
wealth.

'Bread'
When your ambitions cut you off from reality, this is the
one to reach for.

'On Mental Husbandry'
When constantly romanticising and fantasising is your
drug of choice. Not a full cure for love addiction but
certainly a consolation.

'The Settle'
When you are tempted to give up.

'To Another's Perfection'
A spell to cast out envy or excessive awe.

'Chapter'
When you need strength to walk away from an abusive person or situation.

'Love Sickening Still'
When your love addiction kicks in hard it's good to know that there are reasons.

'Slowly Summer On A Step'
When it feels as if the world is going too fast for you.

'The Lazarus Device'
To encourage you when coming out of a funk and back to full power.

'The Visit'
For when someone from the past visits your dreams but not to stay.

'On Standing Too Close'
For anyone who has been parted from a dear one for decades.

'Billy Liar'
If reality is just too much.

'Concert'
If you used to go to gigs, get messy and take risks and these days feel less like your true self than you did before.

'Whenever You Seem To Be Gone'
Missing someone can hurt a little less when you realise they are just in another room right now.

'On Besieging Being So Besieged'
 When you'd love to fill your days with something other than lustful desire.

'Gladly'
A lullaby just for you.

'Unfixed Rates Of Interest'
A celebration of your no longer giving yourself to the lowest bidder.

'Wanting For Word'
When you are desperate for someone to get in touch.

'Flock'
When you need to remember that there are gifts and signs everywhere.

'Boy Writer'
For anyone disappointed in another's wilful (albeit stylish) self-destruction.

'Codependent Hobbies'
In case you'd like a quick smile at your own follies and conditioning.

'Blanket Fort'
You've been hiding for too long, and you know this.

'On The Keeping Of People'
When you need to be reminded of your inherent value and that of others.

'Home'
If you are tired from putting on a good show about being sorted and constantly happy.

'The Folden'
For you if you feel chronically unseen and uncelebrated.

'Worm Inside'
To calm chronic anxiety.

'The Body And Her Dog'
For those in need of cellular healing and recovery from childhood emotional trauma.

'Advancing Hearts'
For those in need of a large shot of pure hope.

NOTES

'A Letter of Poor Apology'
In earlier decades The Ballymun Flats were the focus of
outrage over public housing standards. More recently
many of the Repeal The 8th organising occurred along
Capel Street in the City Centre. The Yeatsian homages
in this poem are intentional.

'The Lady of the Merrion'
The Merrion Hotel in Dublin consists of 3 Georgian
houses and sits opposite Dáil Éireann. Politicians regular-
ly meet at the hotel's Number 23 Bar while in an adjoin-
ing living room hangs a portrait of an unknown lady by
Sir John Lavery RA RSA RHA.

ABOUT THE POET

Judymay Murphy is the granddaughter of Ireland's celebrated Irish poetry scholar and University College Dublin Professor of Celtic Studies, Gerard Murphy, and although he passed away a decade before she was born she would sink into the family edition of his *Early Irish Lyrics* from a young age. She is a regular expert guest on BBC and other radio and TV stations around the globe and still speaks on stages to thousands worldwide several times a year. She successfully immersed herself in Trinity College Dublin for seven years, emerging with a BA Hons. in Drama and a Masters in Literature.

ACKNOWLEDGEMENTS

Heartfelt thanks to Todd Swift and the Eyewear team –
especially designer Edwin Smet and Alex Wylie for his
supportive editing.

Lifelong gratitude to Stolly's in Paris, The Merrion
Hotel in Dublin, the Hay Adams Hotel in DC, and The
Groucho Club in London for being the inspiring and
welcoming places where many of these poems were
written.

To the various poetry nights in the International Bar
on Dublin's Wicklow Street, to Busboys and Poets in
Washington DC, to The Poetry Cafe and Apples and
Snakes in London – where many of these poems were
first performed. Big Love to the people who form the
communities around these evenings for your courage,
creativity and warm listening.

Personal gratitude to Melanie Coffin, Dr Brian
Singleton, Dr Anne Marie D'Arcy, Tigger!, Yury
Revich, Aidan Murphy, Stuart Clarke, Penny Arcade,
Quentin Crisp RIP, Anita Andersen, Brendan Kennelly,
Michael Clayton McCarthy, Tom Tully, Jeff Michalski,
Jane Morris, Danny Breen RIP, Always M, Bernie Katz
The Prince Of Soho RIP, Lana Citron, Sophie Parkin,
Brian F. Martin, Paul Doherty, All at BBC London, Julie
Keywell, Christine Nagy, Rita Godfrey, Jeff Cannon,
Naomi Fawcett, Vicki St George and the TR family,
The Groucho Early Morning Mob, Danny and Sadie
Coll, Sr Rose Elizabeth, Clodagh O'Donoghue, Helen
O'Hanlon and those whom I will soon be embarrassed
for having omitted to mention. A village indeed.